WOMAN TO WOMAN: DAILY MOTIVATIONAL QUOTES

BY DR. CIERRAH PERRIN

I dedicate this book to
Ms. Barbara Ann Smith and
Ms. Betty Ann Perrin – two strong
matriarchs of their families.

Foreword

I'd spent most of the morning in bed, sulking about the events from two nights prior. At this moment, I felt alone, as I often did. I'd skipped church, unable to muster the energy to go. Sleep – my getaway, my light at the end of the tunnel, but also my detriment – seemed to provide me with some sense of sanity. I hadn't showered in two days; however, my obligations for the day required it. The prior day had been hot, sticky, and muggy. I needed to wash the day off, and I needed to wash the day – in fact, the weekend – away. I hadn't yearned for a Monday in this way before – a fresh start. As I undressed in front of the bathroom mirror, I lifted my arms where, to my surprise, purple bruises had begun to appear. Reminders of the events from two nights earlier. The anger, the terror, the feeling of hopelessness.

I think we've all been there, in ugly situations – the unspeakable ones, the unbearable ones. But what I learned is that it's always just one foot in front of the other. I keep going because it's only when I fail to move, when I fail to make sense of life, when I fail to choose life, that the self–love I proclaim to have for myself begins to waver.

Often, we engage in a constant battle with our very own thoughts. Scenarios we make up, problems we find. These things, all counterproductive, have no place in our lives. So, who are you? Whose are you? Who do you want to be? I have battle scars, too. They`re ugly but they`re mine. I decided to love them, as they help make me who I am. A discolored story, on discolored skin, engrained in my belly, rigid and rough. In this season, a season of endurance, a season of hope, a season of reflection, a season of growth, it`s time to let go of what was and to accept what is. We know we can`t ignore the experiences that shaped us but we can take the time to acknowledge a job well-done, even if we aren`t at the finish line yet. This is what I affirm to you, woman to woman.

Loving yourself is: embracing your flaws, the bad, the ugly, the unspeakable, and the unbearable.
—Dr. Marquita Taylor

Table of Contents

January – 31 days:

THE MONTH OF ACCOUNTABILITY

January 1st

~~~

Let this be your selfish year.
This is your "I gotta get myself together"
year. This should be your self-care year.
This is your know-your-worth year.
This is your level-up year.
This year belongs to you!
Take accountability for the life you are
meant to have.

January 2nd

~~~

Listen to the silence.
It has so much to say.
Your response is your
responsibility.
Saying nothing is saying
something.

11

~~~

January 3rd

~~~

A huge amount of freedom comes to you when you take nothing personally.

12

~~~

January 4th

~~~

You can pursue your dreams, or you can pursue drama, but you can't do both. Pick a side.

13

~~~

January 5th

~~~

You must trust that the seeds
you are planting will manifest.
If you don't believe in yourself,
the universe won't, either.

14

~~~

January 6th

~~~

Drama doesn't just walk into your life. Either you create it, you invite it, or you associate with it.

~~~

January 7th

~~~

Work on being in love with the person in the mirror who has been through so much but who is still standing.

~~~

WOMAN TO WOMAN: DAILY MOTIVATIONAL QUOTES

January 8th

~~~

Accountability feels like an attack when you're not ready to acknowledge your behavior!

17

~~~

January 9th

~~~

Express how you feel and don't ever apologize for being real about your emotions.

~~~

WOMAN TO WOMAN: DAILY MOTIVATIONAL QUOTES

January 10th

~~~

Your competition isn't other people. Your competition is: your procrastination, your ego, your unhealthy relationships, the knowledge that you neglect to learn, the negative behavior you're nurturing, and your lack of accountability.

19

~~~

January 11th

~~~

When you're not the same person you used to be, you have no business going where you used to go.

~~~

WOMAN TO WOMAN: DAILY MOTIVATIONAL QUOTES

January 12th

~~~

No matter how wrong it was, no matter who wasn't there for you, don't use it as an excuse to live bitter, to give up on a dream.

21

~~~

January 13th

~~~

Take accountability for putting yourself in certain situations.

January 14th

~~~

Negativity can affect you only if you are on the same frequency. Vibrate higher.

23

~~~

January 15th

~

Not all storms
come to disrupt your life.
Some come to clear your path.

January 16th

~~~

When you can't control what's happening around you, challenge the way you respond to what's happening. When things are out of your hands, you are still responsible for yourself.

25

~~~

January 17th

~~~

There are years when you ask questions and years when you get answers. Recognize what year you are in. Don't sacrifice being valuable just to be visible.

~~~

WOMAN TO WOMAN: DAILY MOTIVATIONAL QUOTES

January 18th

~~~

Be selective with your battles. Sometimes peace is better than being right. What screws us up the most in life is the picture in our heads of how things are supposed to be.

27

~~~

January 19th

~~~

Freedom is knowing yourself beyond your story. You don't have to be perfect to inspire others. Let people take inspiration from how you deal with your imperfections.

28

~~~

January 20th

~~~

You cannot correct what you
are unwilling to confront.

~~~

January 21st

~

The art of being wise is knowing who to ignore, what to overlook, where to leave things, when to move on, and why it's necessary.

~

WOMAN TO WOMAN: DAILY MOTIVATIONAL QUOTES

January 22nd

~~~

Make sure you are not
the weapon formed against
yourself—the one that is
preventing you from prospering.

~~~

WOMAN TO WOMAN: DAILY MOTIVATIONAL QUOTES

January 23rd

~~~

It's not about perfect. It's about effort. When you bring effort every single day, transformation takes place. That's how change happens.

~~~

WOMAN TO WOMAN: DAILY MOTIVATIONAL QUOTES

January 24th

~~~

Five things to give up:
1. Overthinking
2. Fear of change
3. Living in the past
4. Negative self-talk
5. Trying to please everyone!

33

~~~

January 25th

~~~

Inner peace is the new success. Don't allow anyone to take that away from you. Eliminate what doesn't help you evolve.

~~~

January 26th

~~~

There is no competition
when you are manifesting in
your own lane.

~~~

January 27th

~~~

Be the type of energy that allows you, no matter where you go, to always add value to the spaces and lives around you.

36

~~~

WOMAN TO WOMAN: DAILY MOTIVATIONAL QUOTES

January 28th

THE MONTH OF ACCOUNTABILITY

Just get better, Sis ... every day.
Learn from losses.
Celebrate wins.

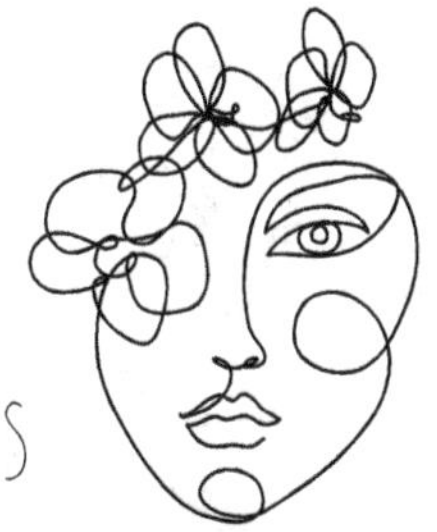

January 29th

~~~

The fact that you aren't where you want to be should be enough motivation.

~~~

January 30th

~~

Girl, YOU got this!
Don't give up, okay?
The next season is personal.
No one—not even YOU—
can get in your way!

39

~~

January 31st

~~~

You're never too young to start an empire or too old to start a dream. The only people who are mad at those making moves are the ones who are standing still.

40

~~~

My Thoughts

My Thoughts

WOMAN TO WOMAN: DAILY MOTIVATIONAL QUOTES

February – 28 days:

THE MONTH
OF FRIENDSHIP

February 1st

~~~

You cannot make someone understand a message that they are not ready to receive.

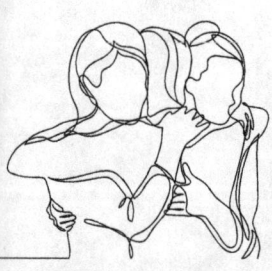

44

~~~

February 2nd

~~~

If you hang out, or associate yourself, with someone who is doing or who does wrong, and if you have full knowledge of it, you're no longer an innocent bystander.

45

~~~

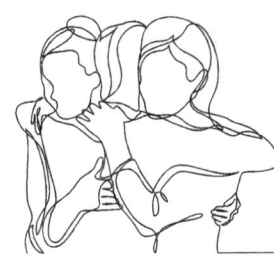

February 3rd

~~~

Let's stop taking people's absences so personally. Sometimes what they're going through requires isolation. It's not even about you!

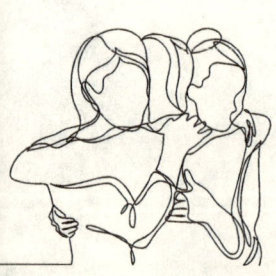

46

~~~

February 4th

~~~

Better get you a friend who
can pray you through your
mess instead of one who keeps
you in that mess.

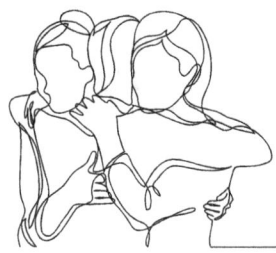

47

~~~

February 5th

~~~

You don't truly know
a person until they don't
get what they want.

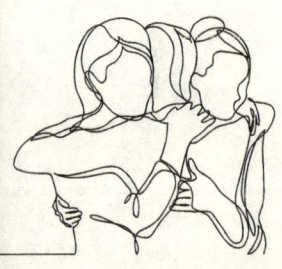

~~~

WOMAN TO WOMAN: DAILY MOTIVATIONAL QUOTES

February 6th

~~~

Let it come calmly and naturally.
Let it go calmly and naturally.
Don't force a connection.
You must be able to have fewer
pointless conversations and
more comfortable silences.

49

~~~

February 7th

~~

Friendship isn't always 50/50. Some days, your friend will struggle. A good friend will suck it up and buck up the 80/20 because they need you ... and you have no doubt that they would do the same for you.

50

~~

February 8th

~~~

Healthy friendships are important.
No competing, jealousy,
gossip, or any other negativity.
Learn to be a good friend
and surround yourself
with good people.

51

~~~

February 9th

~~~

You cannot talk butterfly language around caterpillar people. To effectively communicate, we must realize that we are all different in terms of the way we perceive the world. We must use this understanding to guide our communication with others.

52

~~~

February 10th

~~~

Never forget the people
who take time out of their day
to check on you. The dopest
sh*t ever is mutual love.

53

~~~

February 11th

~~~

Reactions are your greatest source of wisdom about people. When you tell someone good news and you feel the conversation get dry, pay attention to that sh*t.

54

~~~

February 12th

~~~

The right person by your side
will have you saving money,
living better, making moves,
and laughing constantly.

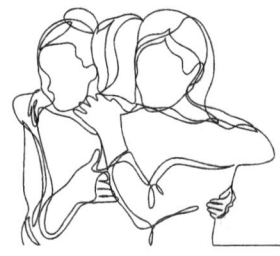

55

~~~

February 13th

~~

Sometimes, during a small
misunderstanding,
the universe exposes how
people feel about you.

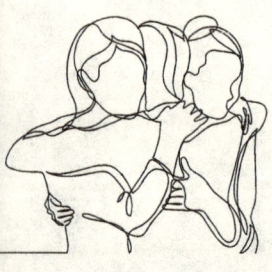

56

~~

February 14th

~~~

Do yourself a favor and stop going around people who don't like you. It doesn't matter if they're family or not.
Live in peace!

57

~~~

February 15th

~~~

Vibes speak louder than words.
Energy is such a dry snitch.

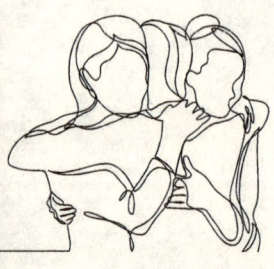

~~~

February 16th

~~~

Get yourself a best friend
who will love you when
you don't know how to love
yourself—one who will stick
by your side even if you make
shitty decisions.

59

~~~

February 17th

~~~

You can never build a kingdom with someone who still craves attention from the village.

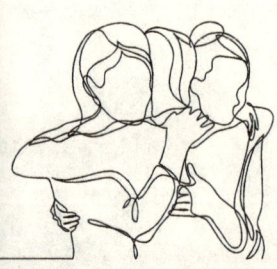

February 18th

~~~

Be good to people. You will be remembered more for your kindness than for any level of success you could possibly gain.

61

~~~

February 19th

~~

Communication is NOT the key to a successful relationship. Comprehension is. It really doesn't matter how much you communicate with a person if they don't get sh*t. In that case, what good is communication?

62

~~

February 20th

~~~

You didn't do anything wrong.
All you did was grow,
and they got mad.

~~~

February 21st

~

Be careful not to loan out what you may need back. I'm not talking about money. Your time. Your energy. Your loyalty. Your love.

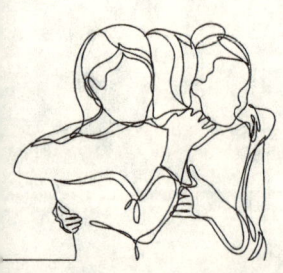

64

~

February 22nd

~~~

Spend time with people who are good for your mental health.

65

~~~

February 23rd

~~~

You can be friends with someone for years and it could take years before you realize that they were never your friend.

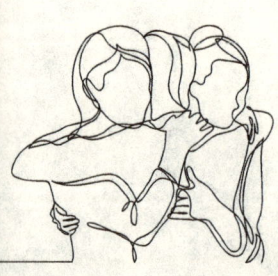

66

February 24th

~~~

Your friend's friend who isn't your friend should never know your business!

~~~

February 25th

~~~

Find someone who speaks your language, so you don't spend a lifetime translating your spirit.

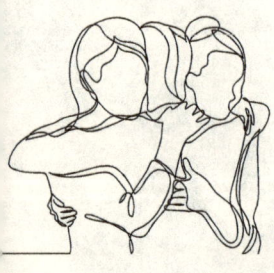

~~~

WOMAN TO WOMAN: DAILY MOTIVATIONAL QUOTES

February 26th

~~~

Some fallouts can
bless your life.

~~~

February 27th

~~~

Not everyone is meant to be in your life forever. The key is to know when to cut them off.

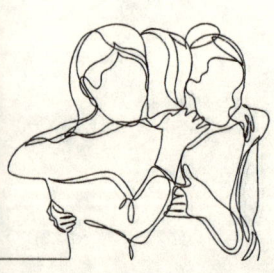

~~~

February 28th

~~~

Sometimes you must distance yourself to save yourself. Not everyone will be loyal to you. Some people enter your life as a reminder to be careful about who you let in your circle.

71

~~~

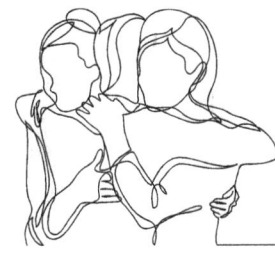

February 29th (Leap Year)

~~~

Support your friends. Listen to their ideas. Go to their events. Buy what they're selling when you can. Share their posts. Celebrate their victories and remind them of their importance after failures. Push them. A little support can go a long way.

72

~~~

My Thoughts

My Thoughts

March – 31 days:

THE MONTH OF
SELF-LOVE

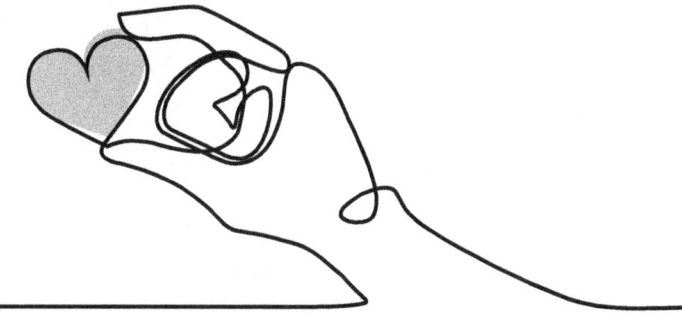

March 1st

~~~

Nobody wants to tell you why discipline is so important. Discipline is the strongest form of self-love. It is ignoring current pleasures for bigger rewards to come. It is loving yourself enough to give yourself everything you've ever wanted.

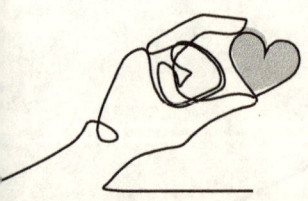

~~~

March 2nd

~~~

You are good enough. Actually, you're overqualified but let's start the month off humble.

~~~

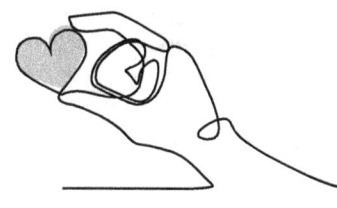

March 3rd

~~~

Be consistent with yourself—
with your actions, feelings, and
thoughts. When you consistently
show up for yourself, you learn
what it means to be consistent with
others and how to walk away from
inconsistent people.

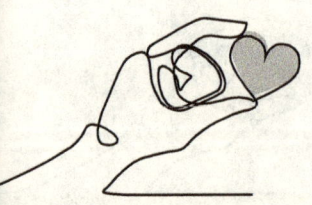

~~~

March 4th

~~~~

You may think the battle is between you and someone else. Nah, the battle is between you and YOU. Life just uses battles to expose what you need to work on.

79

~~~~

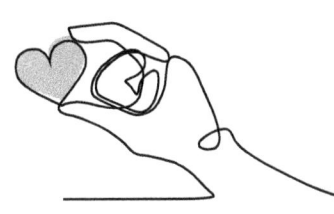

March 5th

~~~

It's so empowering to say,
This isn't serving me, and to
walk away in peace.

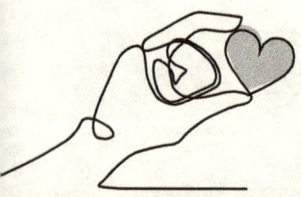

~~~

WOMAN TO WOMAN: DAILY MOTIVATIONAL QUOTES

March 6th

~~~

Energy is neither created nor destroyed, so when your life is in the midst of chaos, something is disrupting the flow.

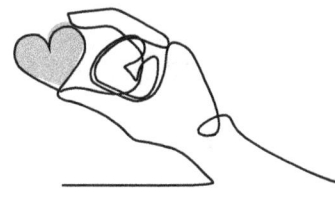

~~~

March 7th

~~~

Understanding spiritual maintenance is mandatory.

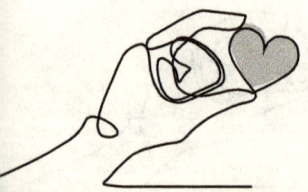

~~~

March 8th

~~~

Self-love: calling yourself out
on your sh*t in order to grow.

~~~

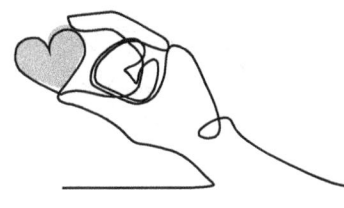

March 9th

~

If you understand how frequently people cope by projecting, you'd learn to take absolutely nothing personally.

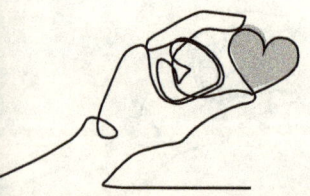

~

March 10th

~~~

I'm so proud of all of us who are correcting dysfunction from childhood, ridding ourselves of toxicity, and healing. Trusting the process that it gets better. It takes time and dedication and it's not easy to unlearn behaviors, habits, and emotional trauma.
Keep pushing.

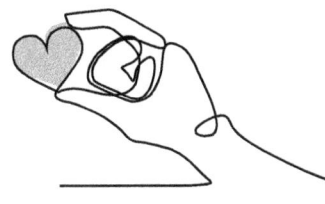

85

~~~

March 11th

~~~

Look at you, glowing with
self-love and becoming a
magnet for good vibrations.
I'm proud of you.

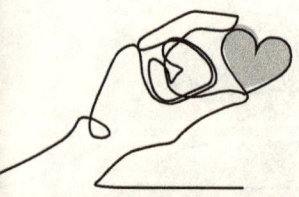

March 12th

~~~

If a person always leaves you with mixed feelings, uncertainty, and an unsettled mind, you don't need to place your energy there.

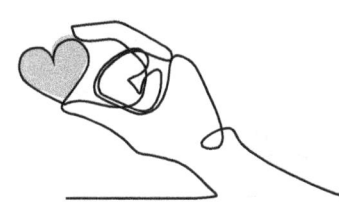

~~~

March 13th

~~~

Don't be afraid to start over.
This time, you aren't starting
from scratch; you're starting
from experience.

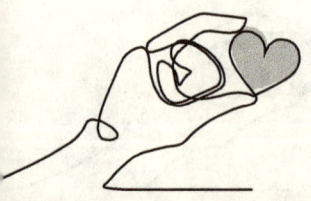

88

~~~

March 14th

~~~

Life always works out.
Things always turn out in your favor,
even if they don't follow the original
plan. Find comfort in knowing that all
you're currently experiencing is a
transition and transformation period
that will lead to bliss and abundance.

89

~~~

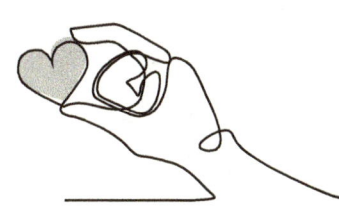

March 15th

~~~

If it's for you, it will come to you. No chasing, no anxiety, and no stress. What's for you can never pass you by. Trust the process.

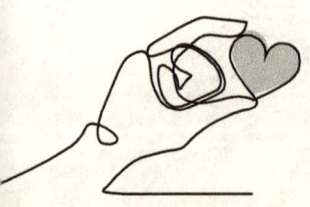

~~~

March 16th

~~~

You gotta stop telling good
news to bad spirits.
Read that again.

~~~

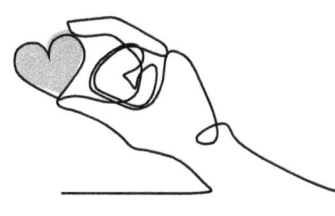

March 17th

~~~

Make it a habit of shutting down conversations that involve hating on other people.

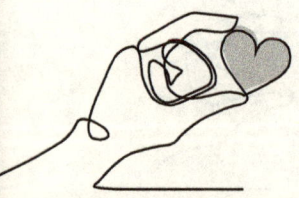

~~~

March 18th

~~~

If you can't be corrected
without being offended,
you'll never grow.

~~~

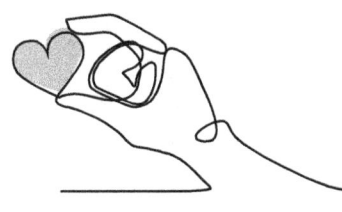

March 19th

~~~

Sometimes you have to temporarily close yourself for spiritual maintenance. Knowing when you need self-care is the first step.

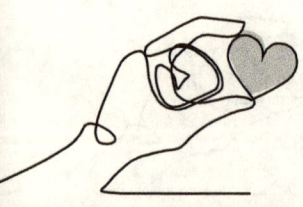

~~~

March 20th

~~~

Wake up tomorrow. Eat a good
breakfast. Do your hair and makeup and
put on a kick-ass outfit. Buy your cup
of coffee and enjoy every sip of it.
Get to work, make that money, and
learn something new in the process.
Nourish. Grow. Inspire.
Self-destruction is not an option.

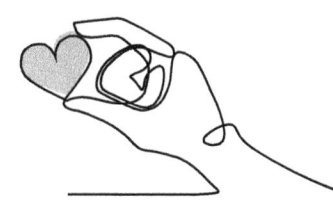

95

~~~

March 21st

~~~

It's crazy but working on yourself never ends. You get better and ... boom. Now it's new sh*t you gotta work on. You just keep unlocking endless levels of growth.

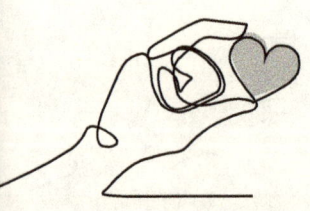

96

~~~

March 22nd

~~~

Look in the mirror.
Figure out what you need.
Give it to yourself.

97

~~~

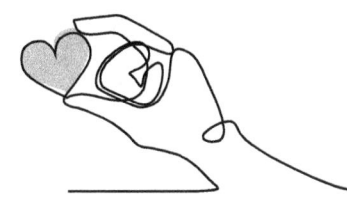

March 23rd

~~~

At some point, you have to look at certain people and certain situations and know, in your heart, that you didn't lose them. Rather, they lost you. When you've been really good, when you've loved hard, and when you've been nothing but devoted, you can walk away in peace.

98

~~~

March 24th

~~~

Sometimes you fall off the wagon for months. Sometimes you tell yourself that you're going to start fresh on Monday and by Wednesday you've already fallen back off. Sometimes you have to restart 100 times and it's frustrating. But it'll be okay. You can do this. One day at a time.

99

~~~

March 25th

~~~

It never gets easier.
You just get better.

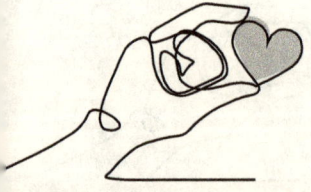

~~~

March 26th

~~~

It takes a strong woman to
sit down with herself, calm her
storm, and heal all of her issues
without trying to bring someone
else into that chaos. Your
journey to self-love is just
that—and you're doing it.

101

~~~

March 27th

~~~

Your mental health should be a priority over any friendship or relationship. Be willing to lose anyone or anything before you lose your mind.

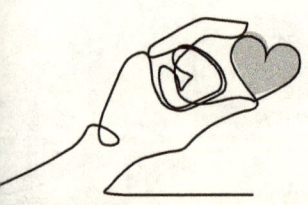

~~~

March 28th

~~~

When you finally walk away from something that wasn't good for you, you start to attract all the things that were meant for you.

103

~~~

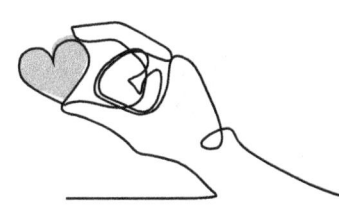

March 29th

~

A lot of things will break your heart but fix your vision. Self-love brings you clarity, not confusion. Go back within yourself for clarity and answers.

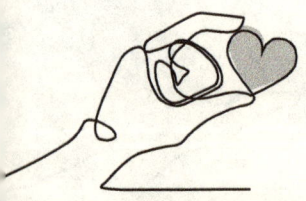

~

March 30th

~~~

Nothing is more beautiful than
a woman coming back to herself.

105
~~~

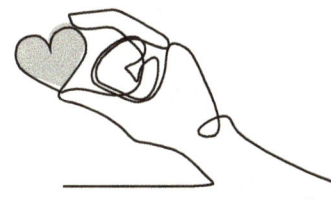

March 31st

~~~

You don't need more advice.
You need to trust yourself
more. Your growth owes no
one an explanation.

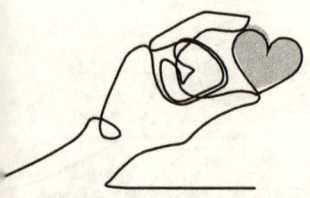

106

~~~

My Thoughts

My Thoughts

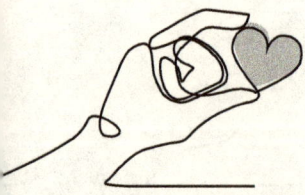

April – 30 days:

THE MONTH
OF LOVE

April 1st

~~~

Never beg to be loved.
Sometimes a person doesn't
love you; they just love the way
you love them.

April 2nd

~~~

Your taste in people
will change when you learn
to love yourself.

April 3rd

~~~

You must accept what and
who is not for you,
the same way you accept what
and who is for you.

April 4th

~~~

You can't date the potential you see in someone and then get mad when they don't live up to be the person you thought they should be.

April 5th

~~~

Someone can love you desperately with their feelings and still not know how to love you correctly with their actions.

April 6th

~~~

Stop providing wifely benefits on a girlfriend's salary.

April 7th

~~~

One man's *I'm not ready* is another man's *I knew the moment I saw her.*

116

April 8th

~~~

The biggest rule in a relationship is this: No matter how mad you are at your partner, don't go out and seek someone else's attention. If that's who you truly love, sit your ass down and make it right.

April 9th

~~~

You owe yourself the biggest apology for putting up with sh*t you didn't deserve.

WOMAN TO WOMAN: DAILY MOTIVATIONAL QUOTES

April 10th

~~~

It'll never be perfect but if it's
what your heart desires,
and if it's good for your soul,
you'll make it work.

April 11th

~~~

The whole *I don't care* act is dead and tired. If you're dealing with someone who doesn't have emotions, cool. Tell them to seek therapy or be toxic somewhere else.

WOMAN TO WOMAN: DAILY MOTIVATIONAL QUOTES

April 12th

~~~~

As you get older, you can energetically feel the difference between people who love you and people who care about you at their own convenience.

April 13th

~~~

Stop holding on to
who he was supposed to be.
He lied, Sis. Move on.

122

April 14th

~~~

Good intentions don't excuse
bad decisions.

April 15th

~~~

Love isn't a contest to see how much pain you can withstand. How many burdens you can carry. How many untrustworthy situations you can jump over in the hope that maybe one day he'll do right.

124

April 16th

~~~

Don't dumb it down for anyone.
Make them come up and get it.

April 17th

~~~

A commitment-phobe will stick around for a woman who will give her all without requiring him to do the same. Don't be that woman.

April 18th

~~~

Sometimes the weight you need
to lose isn't on your body.
Read that again.

April 19th

~~~

Forgive yourself for loving the wrong person. You know better now.

April 20th

~~~

Tell yourself, *Dear soul, I'm still learning about what you love. I'm going to give us more of that, I promise.*

April 21st

~

Stop chasing people and being the
only one trying to fix everything.
It's mentally and physically exhausting.
You must find peace with whoever
comes and goes from your life.
Don't be the only one putting in the
effort, If you do, you will lose yourself
while trying to save someone else.

130

April 22nd

~~~

Until men and women start having honest conversations about who they truly are, what demons they battle with, where they lack, where they come from, and what they really want, love will continuously be a temporary emotion. Honesty and communication are key.

131

April 23rd

~~~

It's important to realize that no matter how good you are to people, it won't make them good to you.

April 24th

~~~

Work on things people can't take from you—things like your character, your personality, your transparency ... your entire being.

133

April 25th

~~~

You're about to enter a relationship that only God can take credit for.

April 26th

~~~

Fall in love with someone who never lets you fall asleep feeling unwanted.

April 27th

~~~

Aye, if you gotta thug it out by yourself, do that!

April 28th

~~~

You must train your mind to be stronger than your emotions. Otherwise, you'll lose yourself every time.

April 29th

~~~

Sometimes your heart needs
more time to accept what your
mind already knows.

April 30th

~~~

Know your worth, then add local and federal taxes, shipping and handling, and cancellation and processing fees. If you allow people to make more withdrawals than deposits in your life, you'll soon end up in the negative. Learn when to close the account.

139

My Thoughts

May – 31 days:

THE MONTH
OF SUCCESS

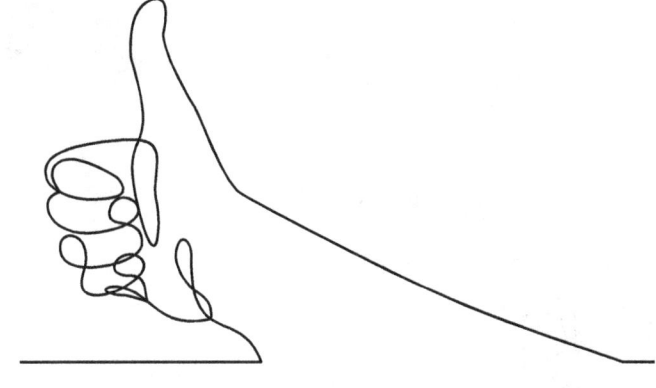

May 1st

~~~

If you can't figure out your purpose, figure out your passion. Passion will lead you right to your purpose.

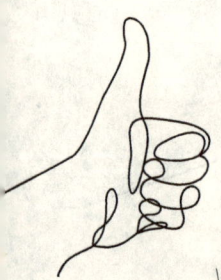

~~~

May 2nd

~~~

Sis, the success of other women does not cancel out your own. Stop being bitter towards another woman's blessings. Instead, focus on what you need to do. If you're hating on that queen for what she has, it means you lack faith that God can certainly do it for you, too. Don't dim her light. Every woman in this world can win.

143

~~~

May 3rd

~~~

The only obstacle to your success and achievement is your own thoughts or mental images. Don't let failure take you out. Don't let it discourage you. That door that closed today will lead you to a door with a bigger opportunity tomorrow.

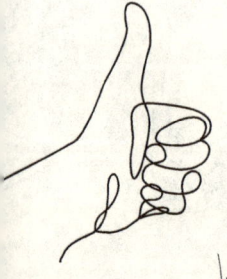

~~~

May 4th

~~~

The blessings didn't come from people, so they can't be taken by people. Almost every successful person begins with two beliefs: 1. The future can be better, and 2. I have the power to make it so.

145

~~~

May 5th

~~~

Deep down, you know exactly what you are capable of. There are even moments when you get a glimpse of all your potential. You can get there. You just have to be willing to sacrifice the habits, things, and situations that are standing in the way of your success.

146

~~~

May 6th

~~~

The greatest gift you can give someone is your own personal development. You are not going to master the rest of your life in one day. Just relax. Master the day. Then keep doing that every day, the best way you can.

147

~~~

May 7th

~~~

Write down what matters to you and what kind of life you want to have. That way, when you encounter opportunities that don't align with your list, you'll know what to say. Sure, you'll get paid, but is it worth it?

148

~~~

May 8th

~~~

Step up your game and never be afraid to say that you struggled.

~~~

May 9th

~~~

The thinking that will take you to the next level will not be the thinking that brought you to this point.

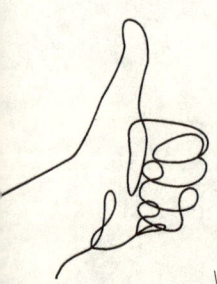

~~~

May 10th

~~~

Leveling up takes periods of
isolation, separation,
and extreme focus.
There's no way around it.

151

~~~

May 11th

~~~

To realize your full potential,
you must never be satisfied with
your last accomplishment.
Be stuck somewhere between
"I'm proud of myself" and
"I gotta go a little harder."

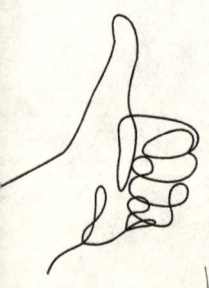

152

~~~

WOMAN TO WOMAN: DAILY MOTIVATIONAL QUOTES

May 12th

~~~

You can't build a solid brand if you aren't perceived as a solid person. It doesn't matter how popular you are. Businesses are successful because of hard work, not popularity.

153

~~~

May 13th

~~~

One day or day one ... you decide. When it involves your life, the choice is always yours.

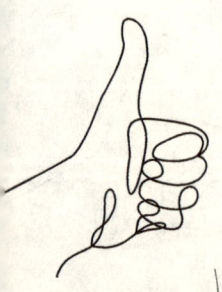

~~~

May 14th

~~~

Never forget who moved funny
while you were getting your
sh*t together.

155

~~~

May 15th

~

A wise woman once said,
"Lack of sleep shows lack of
professionalism." If you truly
cared about your craft and
the vessel that exhibits it (you),
you'd take yo ass to bed.

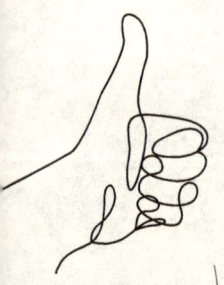

~

May 16th

~~~

Instead of begging for a seat, build your own table. You're not meant to sit with them.

157

May 17th

~~~

Never be in such a rush
for success that you start
to question other people's
blessings.

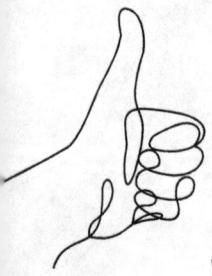

May 18th

~~~

Not everyone is fronting on social media. Some people worked harder than you did. Want more? Do more.

~~~

May 19th

~~~

You can start late, be uncertain, look different, and still succeed.

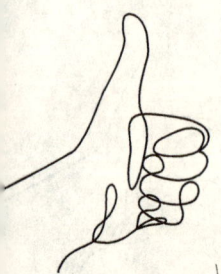

May 20th

~~~

We must get in the habit of telling more people that we are proud of them. Don't associate another person's success with where you are. It's okay to be happy for someone else.

161

~~~

May 21st

~~~

Get in the habit of asking yourself, *"Does this support the life I'm trying to create?"*

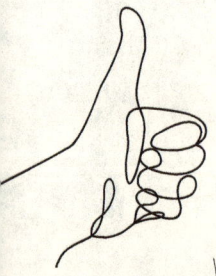

162

~~~

May 22nd

~~~

Part of becoming a successful professional is resisting the urge to respond to emails with "First of all, b*tch..."

163

~~~

May 23rd

~~~

Everything works again after you unplug it for a few minutes and then plug it back in. Apply that to yourself and recharge.

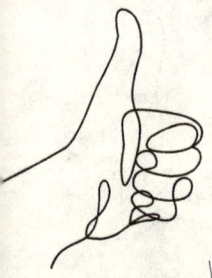

~~~

May 24th

~~~

Obstacles can't stop you.
Problems can't stop you.
Most of all, other people can't
stop you. The only person who
can stop you is you.

165

~~~

May 25th

~~~

Believe in yourself. You'll have to ride off your own gas until it's popular to support you.

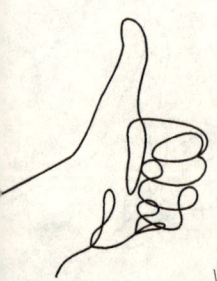

~~~

May 26th

~~~

You have to want it, even on the hard days. Most people think that, to see change, they must move mountains. The truth is, you just need to do better than you did yesterday.

167

~~~

May 27th

~~~

Sometimes the bad things
that happen in our lives put us
directly on the path to
the best things that will ever
happen to us.

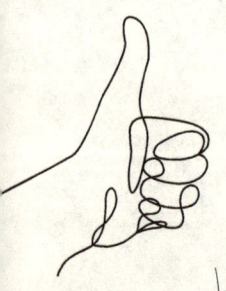

~~~

May 28th

~~~

Getting around the right people is the biggest success hack in the world.

169

~~~

May 29th

~~~

The best career advice that I can give: Don't ever attach yourself to a person, a place, a company, an organization, or a project. Attach yourself to a mission, a calling, a purpose ONLY. That's how you keep your power and your peace.

170

~~~

May 30th

~~~

Some people will hate you just because they see you getting the success they think they deserve from the work they haven't done.

171

May 31st

~

You will never be criticized by someone who is doing more than you are. You will be criticized only by someone doing less. Now read that again.

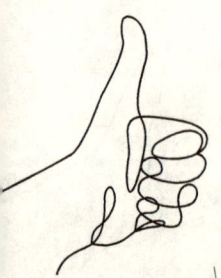

172

~

My Thoughts

My Thoughts

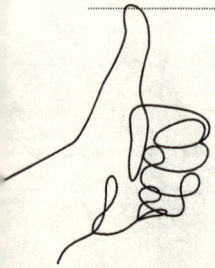

June – 30 days:

THE MONTH OF INSPIRATION AND AFFIRMATIONS

June 1st

~~~

The right time is your time.
Affirm: It's never too late to start and never too late to finish. Getting it done is the ultimate goal. I'm never going to be 100% ready and it's never going to be perfect timing. Every moment is the right moment. I just have to take a leap of faith.

Marieta Milan – Educator
@Nedab__ on IG – Nashville, TN

176

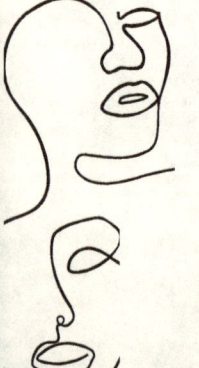

~~~

June 2nd

~~~

Committing to the best version of me. Affirm: I am ready to commit to being the best version of me today. I have infinite powers that radiate self-love, grace, respect, and strength. I am a competent woman and I believe in my abilities. I intend to live the most beautiful life possible and become beneficial to all who meet me because, as women, we are made to create beauty within life in all of its infinite variations.

Dr. Devonne Carney-Brown Ed.D – Professor
@Angelic_01 on IG – Atlanta, GA

177

~~~

June 3rd

THE MONTH OF INSPIRATION AND AFFIRMATIONS

~~~

Forsaken but not forgotten. Within yourself, you will find a person that is determined to rise above all obstacles. Your story may have been filled with broken pieces, you may have made terrible choices, and you may have a lot of ugly truths. However, you will defeat that feeling of abandonment and write a new story that will be filled with hope, courage, and a sense of inner peace.

**Dr. Anesha Fuller Ed.D – Professor, Author,
Founder of No Rest Until Success Foundation
@norestuntilsuccessfoundation on IG – New York, NY**

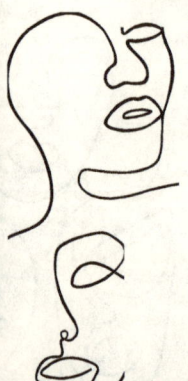

~~~

WOMAN TO WOMAN: DAILY MOTIVATIONAL QUOTES

June 4th

~~~~

Deserving of prosperity. You are deserving of prosperity. Women are sometimes faced with challenges in their life. Where those challenges are connected to financial, familial, professional, or social responsibilities in times of crisis, we have the propensity to question where the dark times that stem from our life choices or unforeseen circumstances make us deserving of prosperity. When life becomes a little bit more difficult and the challenges linger longer than we expected, we find it hard to see the possibilities that await us in our future. Instead of focusing on temporary struggles, we must readjust our vision to capture the potential for greatness that lies within us all. No matter what curve balls life throws at us, it is important to forgive ourselves for the trials and adopt an optimistic view of our future. Be encouraged that we are all deserving of prosperity.

Dr. Jaime Johnson-Duplessis, Ph.D.
– Educational Entrepreneur
@Jaimeduplessis_phd on IG – New Orleans, LA

179

~~~~

June 5th

~~~

Know your limits. Be strong enough to stand alone, smart enough to know when you need help, and brave enough to ask for it. Your mental health is the most important thing. You can't be everything to everyone and that's okay. It's okay to say, No, this is too much. It's okay to break away from anything that takes away from you being you.

TaJuan Givens – Entrepreneur
@Ta.juan on IG – Memphis, TN

180

~~~

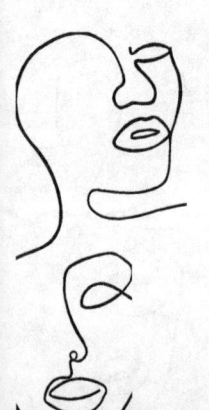

June 6th

~~~

Remember your purpose. Have you looked in the mirror today and realized how amazing you are? Yesterday, last year, or maybe even this morning was tough, but you made it. Remember that bill you thought you couldn't pay, or that man you thought you couldn't get over, or that job that fired you? Look at you now, looking and feeling better than ever. Remember, the journey life takes you on is to prepare you for your purpose—even when you don't understand the directions.

Tamera C. Rogers – Equal Employment Officer, Sr.
@_dalobster on IG – Montgomery, AL

181

~~~

June 7th

~~~

Energy is real. Always be mindful of the energy you convey because the universe certainly has its way. Energy is matched and it's important to know what energy you are projecting so you are aware why certain events happen or how people are responding to you. You can easily mask your expressions or emotions, but the true energy you give off will always be felt.

LaTisha Flye – Entrepreneur and Master Cosmetologist
@forever_flye on IG – Nashville, TN

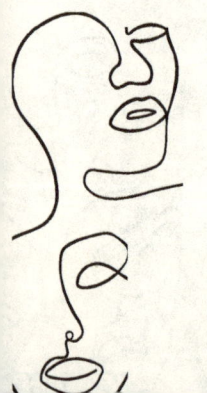

182

~~~

June 8th

~~~

Trust the timing of your life. If there's one mantra that's been important for me to remember throughout my growth in my 20s and development in womanhood, it is to: trust the timing of your life. It's easy to get distracted by what others are doing, to watch opportunities and doors opening for the next person, and sometimes question when it'll be your turn. I promise you, your moment wasn't meant to happen yet. Your moment has yet to be manifested for a reason. Never think that you're in a position of lack. Trust the timing on your life.

Dr. Terri Candace Griffith, Psy.D
– Doctor of Clinical Psychology
@terricandace on IG – Baltimore, MD

183

~~~

June 9th

~~~

Don't forget to enjoy the ride. We spend our entire life trying to control the narrative and we get exhausted by the task. Freedom is when we surrender and allow God to take control of our life. He knows what's best. Relax and enjoy the ride.

Rasheedah Villarreal, MS – National Certified Counselor
@Rasheedah Zalzala on Facebook – Kansas City, MO

184

~~~

June 10th

~~~

Being your authentic self. Coming up in the corporate world consistently being "the only" in the room (the only black person, the only woman, the youngest) could've been a recipe for disaster had I not figured out early on that my success comes from me and being my authentic self. At any point in my life or career when I feel like I am spiraling or losing control, I come back to "be your authentic self." That's your power, that's the key. No one can be you; your path is for you and you only. God specifically gave you unique gifts to align with your purpose. The way you maximize those gifts is in being your authentic self. Don't shrink, hide, or change yourself to make others more comfortable. You should never diminish your light so someone else can shine.

Kimberly Lyons, MPA – Senior
Municipal Credit Analyst
@Glamsquadkrl on IG – Bronx, NY

185

~~~

June 11th

~~~

Shifting the atmosphere. Affirm: I am an atmosphere shifter. Any place I enter is positively affected by me. Anything I put my mind to will reap unimaginable results. Anything I have a hand in will manifest and multiply. My feminine energy has the power to make everything around me work in my favor. I am an atmosphere shifter.

Shennise McLauren – Entrepreneur, Owner of TheHauteShopper @thehauteshopperlps on IG – Atlanta, GA

186

~~~

June 12th

~~~

I will overcome. Affirm: There are no obstacles or barriers that exist in my life that I cannot overcome, as these were predestined to occur for my success and legacy. They are traveling companions on my road to success and will depart upon arrival.

Tiffany Wells, MS – Sociologist and Professor
@ms.sociology on IG – Jacksonville, FL

187

~~~

June 13th

THE MONTH OF INSPIRATION AND AFFIRMATIONS

~~~

I am who I am. Affirm: I am a woman of God, created, designed, and destined to be great through Him. I won't let social culture corrupt me, for I am relevant in my own right. I set my own standards and hold myself accountable for my decisions and actions. Even with the occasional human slip, I will learn from my mistakes and persevere to the best version of myself.

Dr. Kayla Williams – Chiropractor
@dr.k_chiro on IG – Atlanta, GA

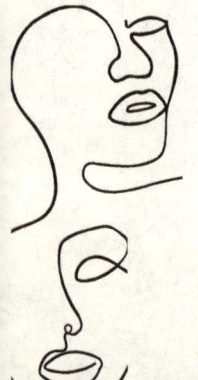

~~~

June 14th

~~~

The truth is expensive, but you're worth every penny. We invest in all things external to ensure that we "look" good. However, in this season, let's explore how we "look" internally. You cannot be your authentic self if you aren't honest about who you are, the things you do, and how you really feel. We demand and expect honesty from everyone except ourselves. You no longer have the luxury to lie to yourself or lie in your mess if your expectation is growth.

Joy Stewart – Life Coach and Entrepreneur, Owner of Glam Luxe Studios @GlamLuxeStudios on IG – Miami, FL | Atlanta, GA

189

~~~

June 15th

~~~

Monitor your inner circle. Sometimes we have relationships with people that we've known forever, and we confuse history with trust, but they are secretly hoping for our downfall. Because they're too scared to live their dreams, they'll attempt to sabotage yours. Watch how certain people react to your good news. Watch how often they ignore your small wins. If their energy starts to feel off, it is. Know who you are dealing with, so their actions won't surprise you. If you're trying to grow, you have to let go.

**LaKesha Welch – Entrepreneur,
Owner of Helen's Hot Chicken
@epitome.of.strength on IG – Nashville, TN**

190

~~~

June 16th

~~~

Be mindful of critics with no credentials. Only take advice from friends in areas of their life that you want to emulate. Example: If you have a friend who's living paycheck to paycheck and makes bad financial decisions, why would you take advice about money from them? On the opposite side, if they've been married for years and have a healthy marriage, then you can take their advice about relationships or marriage. Don't fall in the trap of taking advice from people in your life that aren't qualified on the topic based on their own life.

Jamie Musgrove – Senior Marketing Director
@jamie_e.m.m on IG – Memphis, TN

June 17th

~~~

Being comfortable in your own skin. Affirm: Learn how to be myself. Learn how to smile when people don't like me. Learn how to draw confidence on who I am as a person. Realize that I don't need all the people I thought I needed. I don't need all the support I thought I needed. My plan is bigger than my problems. The whole time, God is teaching and protecting me in the process.

Lameika Gray – Warehouse Payables Lead
@breadwinner_mek on IG – Nashville, TN

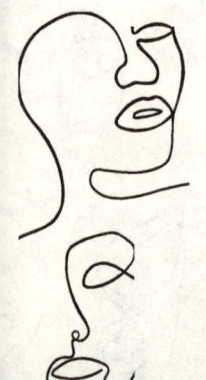

192

~~~

June 18th

~~~~~

Enjoy your ride. Life will not go exactly as you have it planned but work hard for where you want to be. Be grateful for where you are on your journey. Most importantly, have fun along the way. Don't take life too seriously because it can change in the blink of an eye. Living your best life doesn't mean everything is perfect; it means you're happy where you are in life and making the best of it. Life is what you make out of it, so why not buckle up and enjoy the ride?

Dr. Lauren Elise Simpson, Ed.D – CEO of Social Media Dr, LLC, Founder and Executive Director of Adjust Your Crown Mentoring Inc.
@dr.laurenelise on IG – Atlanta, GA

193

~~~~~

June 19th

~~~

Believe in yourself, No one else should believe in you more than you do yourself. The only person that can prevent you from living the life of your dreams is simply YOU. Self-doubt is your biggest enemy. Learn to push the negative thoughts aside and be inspired by everything around you. There will be days when the only person cheering for you is that voice from within.

Sacha Stewart – Style Architect,
Entrepreneur, Branding Expert
@Jamaicansacha on IG – Baltimore, MD

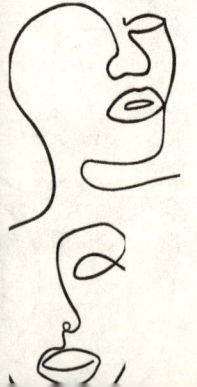

194

~~~

June 20th

~~~~

Be purposely driven. You don't need an audience; all you need is purpose. In this wonderful world of social media, it's important to remain purpose-driven in all that you do. Remember, if their praises feed you, then their criticism will starve you. You had a purpose with your life before anyone had an opinion. Stay true to yourself and trust that your journey is uniquely yours.

Quiana Watson, MBA – Georgia Realtor, Marketing and Branding Expert, Real Estate Agent/Broker at Quiana Watson and Associates @quianawatsonandassociates on IG – Atlanta, GA

195

~~~~

June 21st

~~~

The art of letting go. Knowing when to let go is very vital. So many of us hold on to people that we shouldn't. We feel the uneasiness, the vibe, we see the signs but are afraid to let go. Letting go of someone doesn't mean you have to hate them; it just means you have done what was best for you. It's a painful revelation but you will appreciate your decision more later. Gracefully exit.

Clardia Perrin – Sickle Cell Advocate
@Clardia Perrin on Facebook – Nashville, TN

196

~~~

June 22nd

~~~

Be the driver in your life. Never let anyone remove you from the front seat in life. In order to lead, you must be in the driver's seat. Keep driving with your eyes on the road, staying in your lane. Remember, backseat drivers can't see the greatness ahead.

Rhodina Bly, FNP – Nurse Practitioner
@Rhofab40 on IG – Atlanta, GA

197

~~~

June 23rd

~~~

Manifestation is real. Affirm: I must make a conscious decision to be patient and trust the process. Everything that I have visualized, intended, prayed about and worked towards is in the process of manifesting. Remain centered and at peace. Be strong and believe it's all about to happen to me. Comparison is a thief of joy.

Ashley Goldsby, MS – Family Self-Sufficiency Specialist
@Ashley Goldsby on Facebook – Montgomery, AL

198

~~~

June 24th

~~~~~

Practice radical acceptance. Stop judging yourself and your journey. The time is now that we accept who we are including our struggles and weaknesses. Each of these lessons makes you unique. When you learn to accept the journey, your path will become radically brighter. Three steps that will assist you with radical acceptance are review, reflect, and reset. Reviewing the problem/issue allows you to acknowledge where things may have gone wrong. Reflecting enables you to identify how this problem/issue made you feel. Accepting, you recognize the situation and how it made you feel; you then change how you handle the situation. Radical acceptance is a daily practice. Start with something small.

Dajonay Taylor, MPA
@xdaja on IG – New York, NY

199

~~~~~

June 25th

~~~

Keep the faith. No matter your current walk in life, have faith in God because He'll never give up on you. So, you are not allowed to give up on yourself. Your faith will grow as time passes and fears are removed from within you. That moment will arrive when your faith in God is so strong that you'll know nothing is impossible and everything is possible with God. All it takes is faith of a mustard seed. Find you a mustard seed and carry it daily to remind yourself of the amount it takes. God doesn't ask us for much. Keep the faith even in the hardest of times. You will be rewarded with abundance.

**Sharmeeka Brooks – Serial Entrepreneur
and Motivational Speaker
@_bawselady_ on IG – Miami, FL**

200

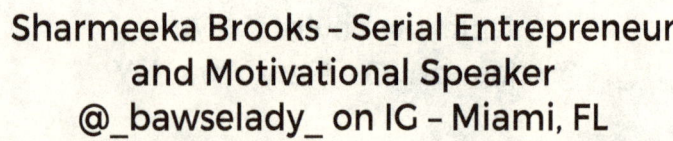

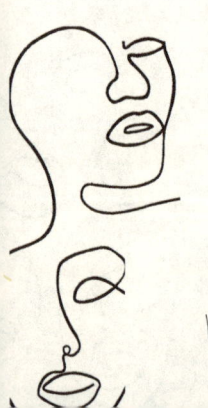

June 26th

~~~

God's will. Know who you are and to whom you belong. As a child of the Most High, always remember the will of God supersedes your own. He will never take you where His grace can't protect you. Before you take on anything new, a relationship or opportunity, be sure to ask yourself if it's God's will. Your vision and dreams should align with the will of God for you to prosper. Once you step out of God's will, for a relationship or opportunity, you must stay there to maintain it. Let that sink in.

Sharry Bain, MS – Executive Assistant/Project Manager
@sharofficialxo on IG – Freeport, Bahamas | Atlanta, GA

June 27th

～～～

Know when to check yourself. You've gotta have an eye out for your mistakes. Once done, it cannot be undone, only corrected and concealed. The key to success is mental. Knowing when self-correction is needed is vital. When you look in the mirror, be proud in knowing that you are taking the necessary steps when no one is looking–the small things that build up your character. Don't self-sabotage your success by ignoring self-correction.

Krissy Le`Slay – Professional Makeup Artist
@Glambosskrissy on IG – Atlanta, GA

202

～～～

June 28th

~~~

Walk with confidence. Make a practice every day of knowing you are enough. Always strive to grow and be better, but know that right now, you are bonafide and certified. Walk with that confidence and nothing can shake you. Life will happen, but confidence will push you through. You're ready!

Dr. Tosha Rogers, MD – OB-GYN
@blackdocruth on IG – Atlanta, GA

203

June 29th

~~~

Manifesting the power of support. My loves, you must always be your biggest supporter. Support yourself not only when no one else will, but also when everyone else does. Use the support system within you to not only support your cause but the cause of others around you as well. It is this generosity of support that will allow you to build yourself up and to build up those who may have not yet discovered that they are, and always should be, their number one supporter.

Sherri J. – Serial Entrepreneur and Childcare Guru
@sherrijlovely on IG – Atlanta, GA

204

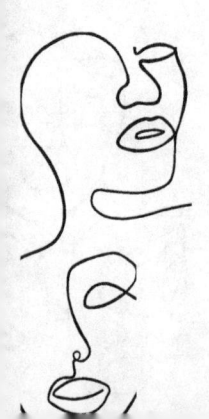

~~~

June 30th

~~~

The uniqueness of your authentic self. You have to always think with your unique mindset, no matter what career path you choose. Always be yourself. Your authentic self. When your energy is natural, you look better, your skin glows, you are intrinsically happier, which in return draws more people towards you. You will look up and realize that your career is booming and you're proud of the person you grew to be. You learned to love – yourself.

**Kesha McLeod – Visual Architect,
Owner @KMCME Agency
@kmcme17 on IG – New York, NY**

205

~~~

My Thoughts

July – 31 days:

THE MONTH
OF FOCUS

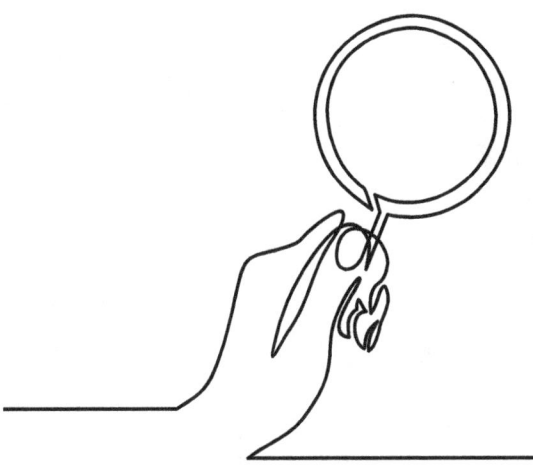

July 1st

~~~

Stop managing your time. Start managing your focus.

~~~

WOMAN TO WOMAN: DAILY MOTIVATIONAL QUOTES

July 2nd

~~~

Don't let failure take you out.
Don't let it discourage you and
don't give up. That door that closed
today will lead you to a door with
a bigger opportunity tomorrow, or
to a window of opportunity beyond
your wildest dreams.

209

~~~

July 3rd

~~~

Consistency is harder when no one is clapping for you. During those times, you must clap for yourself. You should always be your biggest fan.

210

~~~

July 4th

~~~

Ask yourself often:
Am I observing the situation accurately or am I projecting how I feel onto what is happening?

~~~

July 5th

~~~

Struggle is temporary.
Sacrifices are like investments.
Give up the short-term comfort
for the long-term win.
Be patient and stay focused.

212

~~~

July 6th

~~~

Don't stop putting in your best because no one is watching or giving you credit for it. Your defining moment could happen when you least expect it.

213

~~~

July 7th

~~~

How you do anything is how you do everything. Stay focused on how you execute.

~~~

WOMAN TO WOMAN: DAILY MOTIVATIONAL QUOTES

July 8th

~~~

She silently stepped out of the race that she never wanted to be in, found her own lane, and proceeded to win. She is you.

~~~

July 9th

~

When you are not the same person you used to be, you have no business going where you used to go.

~

WOMAN TO WOMAN: DAILY MOTIVATIONAL QUOTES

July 10th

~~~~~

Don't go broke trying to impress other broke people. You can look like money and still not have it. Everybody has a time and a season. We all start from the bottom but it's the work we put in that pushes us further. It's the company we keep that uplifts us. Keeping your priorities in order will help you become financially stable. Make sure you are happy first so that you remain at peace and have the dedication that keeps you focused.

217

~~~~~

July 11th

~

A social media detox every now
and then is necessary.

~

WOMAN TO WOMAN: DAILY MOTIVATIONAL QUOTES

July 12th

~~~

When you are focused
on how good the good is,
the good gets better.

~~~

July 13th

~~~

Don't deny the signs, vibes, and energy you feel about certain people and certain situations. If it's not right, it's not right. Don't lose your focus.

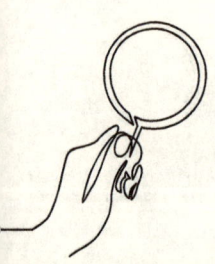

220

~~~

July 14th

~~~

You need to destroy the idea that there's an expectation to do things by a certain age. You don't have to be married with kids at 25. It's okay to not have your dream job at 30 or to not have graduated college by 22. There are no rules to life. It's your race, so go at your own pace.

July 15th

~~~

If you have time to feel like sh*t, complain, and check social media, then you have time to write in your journal, create a list of goals, make a list of things you are grateful for, and better yourself.

222

~~~

July 16th

~~~

Let this be your *nothing can stop me* season.

223

~~~

July 17th

~

You know what's beautiful?
To work on something for
months and to have it manifest
when you least expect it. The
joy you feel when you see the
manifestation in real-time is
unmatched.

224

~

July 18th

~~~

Life is all about your mindset. From the time you wake up to the moment you lay your head on your pillow, every action is dictated by your mindset—your thoughts, your emotions, your perceptions, and your reactions. Every moment.

225

~~~

July 19th

~

Be patient. Everything is coming together. Whatever you are working toward is on its way to you. Stay focused. Remain grateful for your progress.

226

~

July 20th

~~~

Gratitude is a powerful process for shifting your energy and focus.

227

~~~

July 21st

~~~

Be careful about what you focus on. No one is going to stand up at your funeral and say, "She had a really great handbag collection and amazing shoes." Don't make life about stuff.

228

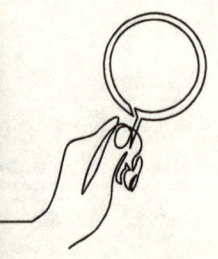

~~~

July 22nd

~~~

The person who challenges you and holds you accountable loves you more than the person who watches you stay the same and settle for mediocrity.

229

~~~

July 23rd

~~~

Stay focused on the results
instead of the recognition.
The right people are
paying attention.

~~~

July 24th

~~~~

Instead of saying that you are stressed, say to yourself, "I am under divine pressure because I'm birthing something great." Create a narrative shift in your focus.

231

~~~~

July 25th

~

Be teachable.
You aren't always right.

July 26th

~~~

We've become so used to
seeing the end result of people
winning materialistically that
we have no idea that winning
spiritually precedes it.

233

~~~

July 27th

~~~

Don't feed your flesh while neglecting your spirit.

~~~

July 28th

~~~

If you could see what's coming,
you wouldn't stress about
what's happening.
Don't lose your focus.

235

~~~

July 29th

~~~

The best math you can learn is how to calculate the future cost of current decisions.

~~~

WOMAN TO WOMAN: DAILY MOTIVATIONAL QUOTES

July 30th

~~~

A major shift is coming.
Stay strong, stay focused,
and stay positive. You will be
flooded with more blessings
than you have room to receive.

237

~~~

July 31st

~~~

It will never be perfect, but make it work.

238

~~~

My Thoughts

My Thoughts

August – 31 days:

THE MONTH
OF FAITH

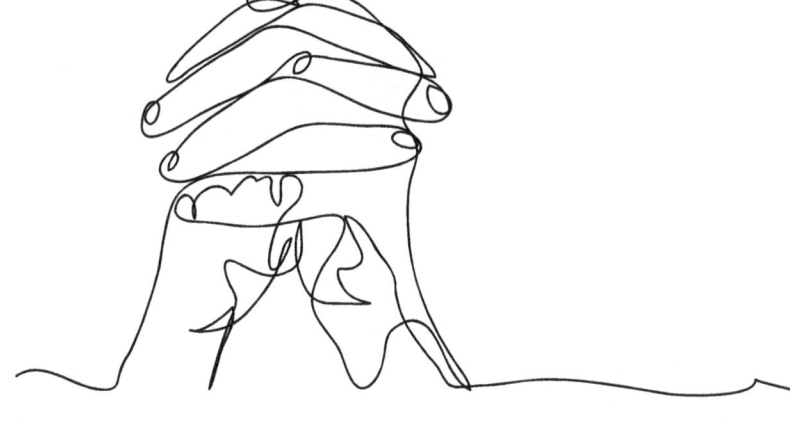

August 1st

~~~

August, September, October, November, and December are going to be some of the most awesome months of your life. More happiness, more love, more blessings, more wisdom.

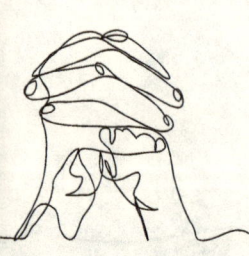

~~~

WOMAN TO WOMAN: DAILY MOTIVATIONAL QUOTES

August 2nd

~~~

Push yourself a little past what you know you can do. Not every closed door is locked. Sometimes you just have to push through.

243

~~~

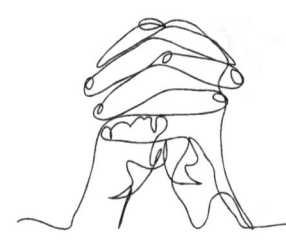

August 3rd

~

Don't be disheartened by your current situation. It may look bleak now but God is working it out for your good. Just continue to do your best.

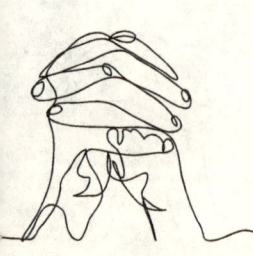

244

~

August 4th

~~~

You might need only one or two really good ideas to change 80% of your life. Figure out what those ideas are and apply them. It's not about knowing every single self-improvement strategy. It's about finding principles that have the biggest impact on your life.

245

~~~

August 5th

~

Stop begging for support and start networking with strangers. There is more than one way to get it. Push through!

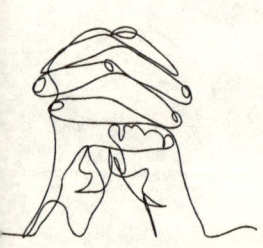

~

August 6th

~~~

Keep working! Someone is telling somebody you're DOPE!

~~~

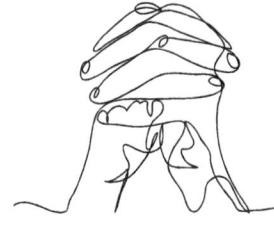

August 7th

~~~

Greater things are coming when everything seems to be going wrong in your life. Old energy is clearing out so that new energy can enter your life.

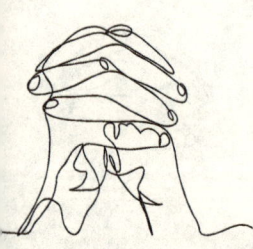

~~~

August 8th

~~~

God has a thousand ways to turn your situation around—ways that you've never even thought of. Just because you don't see a way doesn't mean that God doesn't have a way.

~~~

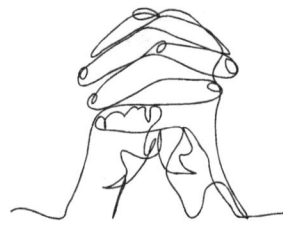

August 9th

~

The more you sweat in practice,
the less you bleed in battle.

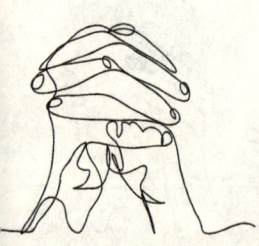

August 10th

~~~

The enemy wouldn't be attacking you if you didn't have something very valuable inside yourself. Thieves don't break into empty houses. You have a purpose!

251

~~~

August 11th

~~~

Where God gives you vision,
He always provides provision.

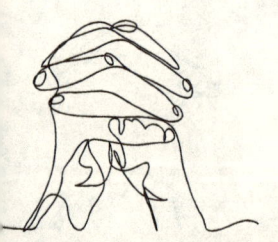

~~~

August 12th

~~~

Often, what we think of as an enemy is really an asset. What we think is there to defeat us is really there to make us better.

253

~~~

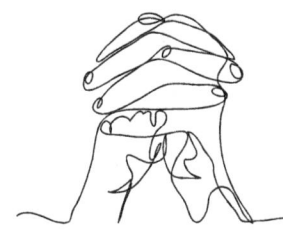

August 13th

~~

You may want God to change
the situation but God wants the
situation to change you.

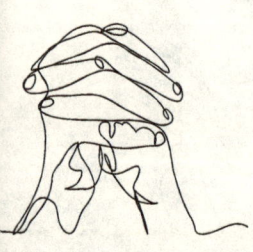

~~

WOMAN TO WOMAN: DAILY MOTIVATIONAL QUOTES

August 14th

~~~

God is retiring the old you to make room for the new you. An upgrade is coming. A new destiny, a new season, and a new purpose will cover your life ... and anyone or anything that interrupts God's plan will be removed.

255

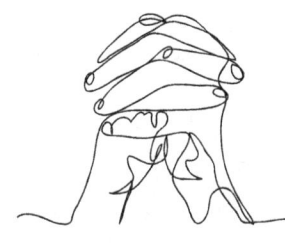

August 15th

~~~

God knows when it's time for you to be seen!

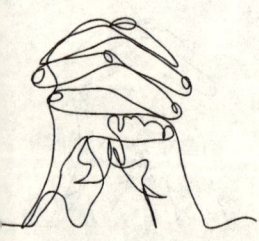

~~~

WOMAN TO WOMAN: DAILY MOTIVATIONAL QUOTES

August 16th

~~~

The dangerous thing about going outside of God's will to get what you want is that you have to stay outside His will to keep it.

257

~~~

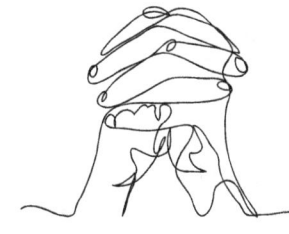

August 17th

~~~

One thing about God is that He'll bring you out of situations that you got yourself into and He won't hold it against you.

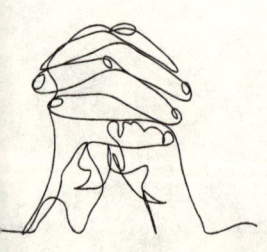

~~~

August 18th

~~~

If you want to reach your destiny,
you have to remove some people
from your inner circle. Your
divine purpose is bigger than you,
your family, and your friends.
God will bring you the right
people to help you grow.

259

~~~

August 19th

~~

Sometimes the miracle is in your staying the course. The outcome was always going to be what God intended. You just had to stay the course.

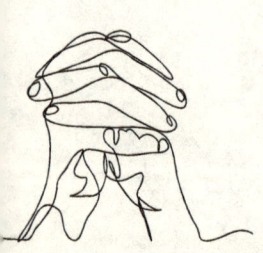

~~

August 20th

~~~

Those seasons when it's just you and God ... they teach you everything.

~~~

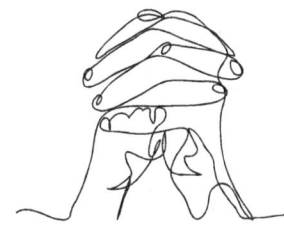

August 21st

~~~

God, I'm all in!

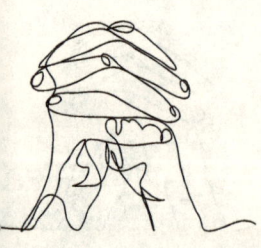

August 22nd

~~~

If you're reading this and if you feel
like you've spent this entire year
praying, believing, expecting,
and patiently waiting for God to
make that one move or open that
one door ... get ready because
He's about to completely
blow your mind!

263

~~~

August 23rd

~

God is never early and
He's never late. He's always
right on time and His plans for
you are for you.

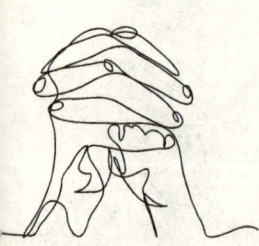

264

~

August 24th

~~~

God is a God of love and order. If the voice you hear doesn't sound like those things, then they aren't from Him.

~~~

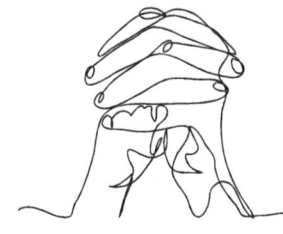

August 25th

~~~

When God doesn't have
your attention,
He will disturb what does.

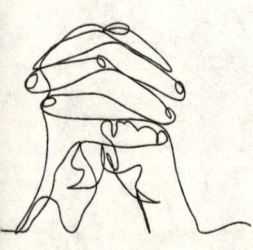

~~~

WOMAN TO WOMAN: DAILY MOTIVATIONAL QUOTES

August 26th

~~~

Sometimes you need to thank God for what didn't happen. Some things were stopped that you know nothing about.

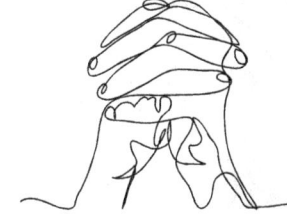

267

~~~

August 27th

~~~

God will put you back
together in front of the people
who broke you.

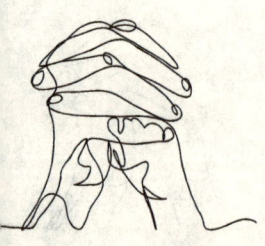

~~~

August 28th

~~~

Stop adding people to your life who have the same characteristics as the people you asked God to remove.

269

~~~

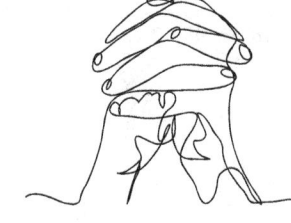

August 29th

~~~

"Nah, bigger." – God. When
you understand the time and
season, you envy no one.

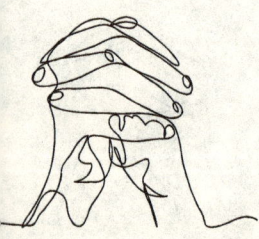

~~~

August 30th

~~~

God didn't give you the strength
to get back on your feet just
so you could run back to
the same thing/person that
knocked you down.

271

~~~

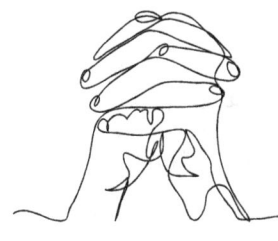

August 31st

~~~

After you receive what you've prayed for, the work to sustain gets real. So, prepare your mind beforehand.

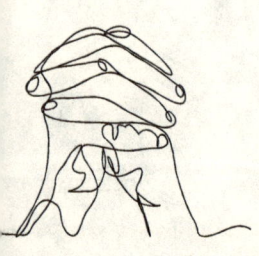

272

~~~

My Thoughts

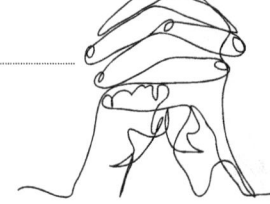

273

~~~

My Thoughts

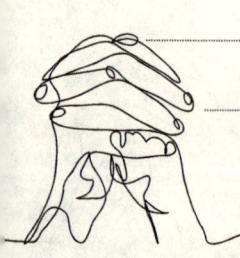

September – 30 days:

THE MONTH
OF STRENGTH

September 1st

~~~

Your greatest strength is the ability to be your highest self even when your lower self is more desired.

~~~

WOMAN TO WOMAN: DAILY MOTIVATIONAL QUOTES

September 2nd

~~~

Whatever battle you may be facing will soon be worth it once you realize your strength and how it carried you through. Don't give up.

~~~

September 3rd

~~

Your next season is going to cause some people to wish they had treated you better in your NOW season.

~~

September 4th

~~~

Have the strength
to let go of people.

279

September 5th

~~~

A shout out to you if you're making progress that no one recognizes because you never let anyone see your darkest moments.

~~~

September 6th

~~~

You've been silently winning battles and transforming yourself; be proud of every step you're making in the right direction. Keep going because you got this!

~~~

September 7th

~~~

Sometimes a change of perspective is all that it takes to transform a painful experience into an empowering growth experience.

~~~

September 8th

~~~

Choose to be patient and trust the process. Everything that you have visualized, intended, or prayed for and worked on is in the process of manifesting. Remain centered and at peace. Be strong and continue to believe.

283

~~~

September 9th

~~~

You owe yourself one hour a day for self-maintenance. This can include reading, writing, yoga, exercise, dancing, meditation, or whatever, but you owe it to yourself. One hour, 1/24 of your day. That's less than 5%. It matters, so make it count.

284

~~~

September 10th

~~~

Sometimes your spirit will tell you to lay low and be patient. Observe and take nothing personally. Rather, take everything for what it is.

~~~

September 11th

~

Stop overthinking or questioning the way things unfold in your life. A certain purpose and timing are attached to everything that is happening in your life, whether good or bad.

~

September 12th

~~~

Those little wins, those
teeny-tiny blessings that pop
up in between the hard days...
that's your confirmation.
Keep going, because
you're back on track.

~~~

September 13th

~~~

You don't have a right to the cards you believe you should have been dealt; you have an obligation to play the hell out of the ones you're holding.

~~~

WOMAN TO WOMAN: DAILY MOTIVATIONAL QUOTES

September 14th

~~~

Strength doesn't come from what you can do. It comes from overcoming the things you thought you couldn't do.

289

~~~

September 15th

~~~

Sometimes deciding
who you are is deciding
who you'll never be again.

~~~

September 16th

~~~

Stop breaking yourself
into bite-sized pieces.
Stay whole and let them choke
off your greatness.

~~~

September 17th

~~~

The universe won't allow you
to move forward until you have
honored where you are now.
Trust your journey.

292

~~~

September 18th

~~~

Just because it hasn't manifested yet doesn't mean it's not on its way to you.

293

~~~

September 19th

~~~

Some people are going
to reject you simply because
you shine too bright for them.
And that's okay. Keep shining.

294

~~~

September 20th

~~~

If you don't like something,
have the strength to take away
its only power: your attention.

295

~~~

September 21st

~~~

Stop worrying about people whom you outgrow. They had a chance to grow with you.

~~~

September 22nd

~~~

You don't give yourself enough credit for overcoming things and getting better. You made it this far. Celebrate your strength.

~~~

September 23rd

~

You can't revive when there's nothing to replenish. Don't run yourself dry—or let anyone else run you dry.

~

September 24th

~~~

Never sit at tables where
you may be the topic of
discussion when you get up.
Respect yourself more.

299

~~~

September 25th

~~~

Can't just be anywhere.
Gotta be where value is valued
and time is respected.

~~~

September 26th

~~~

At a certain age, things are no longer misunderstandings or mistakes. Realize when they are characteristics.

301

~~~

September 27th

~

Never be embarrassed to struggle. There is absolutely no shame in working hard to get where you want to be. There is beauty in your strength.

302

~

September 28th

~~~

Some days are tough but feeling sorry for yourself isn't going to get you where you need to be. So, pick up your passion, strap on your faith, and push forward with determination. Sometimes you must have the strength to save yourself.

303

~~~

September 29th

~~~

Be an adult. Mend relationships that you find valuable. Don't let your pride or your ego destroy good things. However, don't let people play you.

304

~~~

September 30th

~~~

Evolve so hard that they have
to get to know you again.

305

~~~

My Thoughts

WOMAN TO WOMAN: DAILY MOTIVATIONAL QUOTES

October – 31 days:

THE MONTH
OF FORGIVENESS

Sorry

October 1st

~~~

You'll never know how strong you truly are until you have to forgive a person who was never sorry.

Sorry

October 2nd

~~~

Mistakes are painful but, as time goes by, they become a collection of experiences called lessons. Forgive yourself.

309

Sorry

October 3rd

~~~

Be aware of how important
words are in life and the effect
they have on others.
Not everyone will forget
and forgive what you said
during heightened emotional
circumstances.

310

Sorry

October 4th

~~~

No one is obligated to coddle you. Learn to accept empty apologies and silence. Some people are going to make moves that benefit them, not protect you.

311

Sorry

October 5th

~~~

You'll never become who you're really meant to be if you remain attached to who you've been. Forgive yourself and be who you're truly meant to be.

Sorry

October 6th

~~~

When you understand someone's energy, there will never be a need to question their intention.

313

Sorry

October 7th

~~~

You become a more positive, peaceful, and harmonic person when you don't react when people use you as a mirror for their own self-hate.

Sorry

October 8th

~~~

You don't even have to do anything to people these days. They will dislike you just because you carry yourself well.

315

Sorry

October 9th

~~~

Forgiving them is your
gift to them. Moving on is
your gift to yourself.

Sorry

October 10th

~~~

Go fall in love again.
Everyone isn't like him.

Sorry

October 11th

~~~

You deserve people in your life who don't have misconceptions about your personality or intentions.

Sorry

WOMAN TO WOMAN: DAILY MOTIVATIONAL QUOTES

October 12th

~~~

Forgive yourself for not knowing better at the time and for the survival traits and behaviors that you picked up while enduring trauma.

319

Sorry

October 13th

~~~

Before you hold a grudge, hold a conversation. It just may be a result of a misunderstanding.

320

Sorry

October 14th

~~~

Sometimes you have to let people know it's not a grudge you're holding on to. Rather, you're holding onto boundaries.

Sorry

October 15th

~~~

You can forgive a person and never speak to them again. Forgiveness doesn't mean that they are allowed back in your life. It means you've released your attachment to pain.

Sorry

October 16th

~~~

You will come across a lot of toxic people who have a victim mindset. Stay clear of them.

323

Sorry

October 17th

~~~

Don't blame a clown for acting like a clown. Ask yourself why you keep going to the circus.

Sorry

October 18th

~~~

Quit overthinking, replaying failed scenarios, feeding self-doubt, and seeing the good in everyone but yourself. You deserve more.

Sorry

October 19th

~~~

Find the strength to walk away
from a toxic, negative, abusive,
one-sided, dead-end,
low-vibrational relationship
or friendship.

Sorry

October 20th

~~~

Yesterday is heavy.
Put it down.

327

Sorry

October 21st

~~~

The true mark of maturity is when someone hurts you and you seek to understand their situation instead of trying to hurt them back.

328

Sorry

October 22nd

~~~

Chin up, Sis.
You aren't who you were a
year ago. Celebrate that.

329

Sorry

October 23rd

THE MONTH OF FORGIVENESS

~~~

Some people are holding
serious grudges against you
for sh*t they did. Let it go.

330

Sorry

October 24th

~~~

Sometimes we hold on to things/ people so tightly because we're afraid we'll end up empty if we let go. But what if letting go is what frees up your hands to receive what is really meant for you? Something better. Something new. Something you need open hands to receive.

331

Sorry

October 25th

~~~

It sucks to see the true colors of someone you really had love for. Trust what you see.

332

Sorry

October 26th

~~~

Your only limit is your mind. Something that is stressful and painful can make it out of your life. The decision is yours.

333

Sorry

October 27th

~~~

Recognize when a phase, job, life stage, or relationship is over and let it go. Allow yourself to gracefully exit situations you have outgrown. Moving forward doesn't have to be a catastrophic, dramatic event. You can simply move forward with peace and clarity.

334

Sorry

October 28th

~~~

Don't live your life full of regret.
Nothing can be changed,
undone, or forgotten.
Take a lesson, forgive yourself,
and move on.

335

Sorry

October 29th

~~~

Your worst battle is between what
you know and how you feel.

Sorry

October 30th

~~~

Know this: Some people will not hear you no matter how much, how loudly, how truthfully, how lovingly, or how profoundly you speak. Wish them well and let them go.

337

Sorry

October 31st

~~~

Sis, make peace with your past. To love who you are, you cannot hate the experiences that shaped you.

338

Sorry

My Thoughts

Sorry

WOMAN TO WOMAN: DAILY MOTIVATIONAL QUOTES

My Thoughts

Sorry

November – 30 days:

THE MONTH
OF HEALING

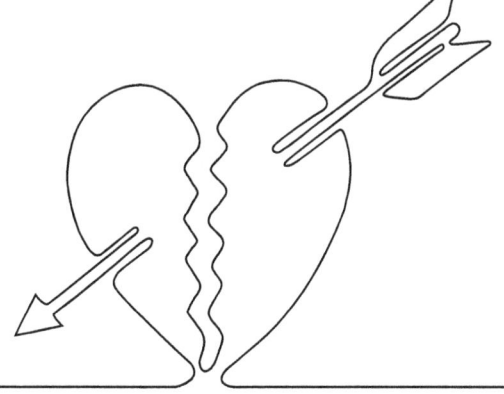

November 1st

~~~

A history of trauma can give you a high tolerance for emotional pain. Just because you can take it doesn't mean you have to or should.

342

~~~

November 2nd

~~~

Once you fully commit to healing, you will understand that people were instruments to aid in your evolution. Focus on the lesson, not the person.

343

~~~

November 3rd

~~~

The soul already knows what to do to heal itself. The challenge is to silence the mind.

344

~~~

November 4th

~~~

You will not heal by going back
to what broke you.

345

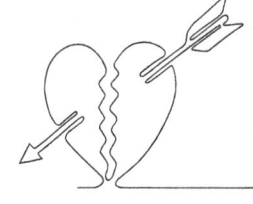

November 5th

~~~

Healing is not something you find. It's something you allow your heart and soul to do.

November 6th

~~~

To find peace, you must be
willing to lose your connection
to the people, places, and things
that create all the noise in
your life.

347

November 7th

~~~

There will be very painful moments in your life that will change your entire world in a matter of minutes. These moments will change YOU. Let them make you stronger, smarter, and kinder. But don't you go and become someone you aren't. Cry. Scream if you have to. Then adjust your crown and keep it moving.

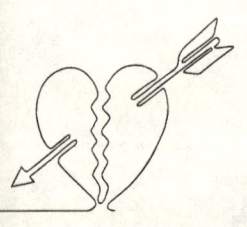

~~~

WOMAN TO WOMAN: DAILY MOTIVATIONAL QUOTES

November 8th

~~~

Everything heals. Your body heals. Your heart heals. The mind heals. Wounds heal. Your soul repairs itself. Your happiness is always going to come back. Bad times don't last.

349

~~~

November 9th

~

Nothing will teach you patience
like trying to heal yourself.

~

November 10th

~~~

One of the most healing things you can do is to recognize and take responsibility when you are your own poison.

~~~

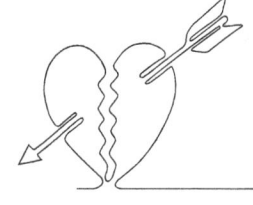

November 11th

~~~

As women, we must heal our broken parts so we can birth whole daughters.

~~~

November 12th

~~~

Until a man heals himself,
he'll be toxic to every woman
who tries to love him.

~~~

WOMAN TO WOMAN: DAILY MOTIVATIONAL QUOTES

November 13th

~

You never know what someone is dealing with behind closed doors. No matter how happy someone looks, how loud their laugh is, how big their smile is, there can be a level of hurt that is indescribable. So be kind, even when others are not. Choose to be kind.

354

~

November 14th

~~~

That ugly part of your story that you've been living through right now will be one of the most powerful parts of your testimony.

355

~~~

November 15th

~~

Your soul is stronger than any trauma you've experienced.

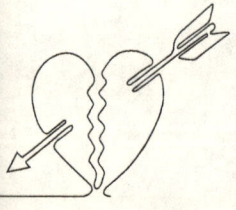

~~

WOMAN TO WOMAN: DAILY MOTIVATIONAL QUOTES

November 16th

~~~

Healing doesn't have to look magical or pretty. Real healing is hard, exhausting, and draining. Let yourself go through it.

357

~~~

November 17th

~~~

An unhealed person can find offense in pretty much anything someone does. A healed person understands that the actions of others have absolutely nothing to do with them. Each day, you decide which person you will be.

358

~~~

November 18th

～～～

Learn to disappear from people's lives. Don't make a scene or confrontation. Just quietly remove yourself. Next thing you know, they'll never be able to get ahold of you again.

～～～

November 19th

~~~

Sometimes you just have
to be done. Not mad,
not upset. Just done!

November 20th

~~~~

People grow when they are loved well. If you want to help someone heal, love them without an agenda.

~~~~

November 21st

~~~

Never trust your tongue while
your heart is bitter.
Wait until you are healed.

~~~

WOMAN TO WOMAN: DAILY MOTIVATIONAL QUOTES.

November 22nd

~~~

If you don't get to the root of family dysfunction and behavior, the generational curses that plague your family will reappear in your children.

~~~

November 23rd

~~~

If you are hurting, you should
be healing, not dating.
Want to be attractive? Heal.

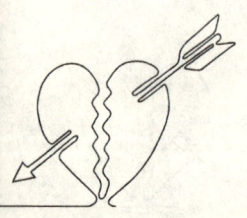

364

~~~

November 24th

~~~

A jealous spirit will cause you to mistreat people who could have been great blessings. Get rid of that hurt and bitter spirit. Heal.

365

~~~

November 25th

~~~

Don't be fooled;
sometimes the healing hurts
more than the wound.

~~~

WOMAN TO WOMAN: DAILY MOTIVATIONAL QUOTES

November 26th

~~~

I see you trying to heal. I'm rooting for you. Don't quit.

367

November 27th

~~~

If the only thing you did today
was to hold yourself together,
I'm proud of you.

November 28th

~~~

Sending love to everyone who's trying their best to heal from things they don't discuss.

~~~

November 29th

~~~

Dear past, thank you for the lessons. Dear future, let's do things differently.

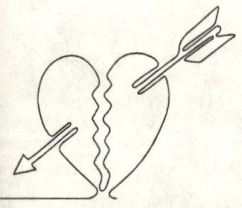

370

~~~

November 30th

~~~

It eventually gets better, without any sort of explanation. One day, you just realize that you're no longer upset. You're no longer mad, hurt, or bothered by things that took up so much of your energy and so many of your thoughts. You will find yourself in a peaceful place and enjoying the feeling of a healed soul.

371

~~~

My Thoughts

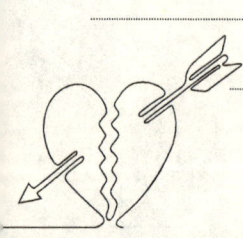

December – 31 days:

THE MONTH
OF HAPPINESS

December 1st

~~~

Don't ever feel bad when you make a decision about your own life that upsets other people. You are not responsible for their happiness. You are responsible for your own happiness. Anyone who wants you to live in misery for their own happiness shouldn't be in your life to begin with.

374

~~~

December 2nd

~~~

Things won't make sense when you're going through a mental, physical, and spiritual transformation. Everything in your life is shifting. You're being upgraded. Something great will come out of it. Don't be afraid or overthink what's happening. With change comes uncertainty, but you have to believe that you're working toward the greater good.

375

~~~

December 3rd

~~~

Happiness over history—you gotta let go of that toxic sh*t.

~~~

December 4th

~~~

The man or woman you choose to be your partner affects everything in your life: your mental health, your peace of mind, the love inside you, your happiness, how you get through tragedies, your success, how your children will be raised, and so much more. Choose wisely.

377

~~~

December 5th

~~~

You say you want to be happy ... but what are you willing to sacrifice? Are you willing to put down the phone? To let go of that toxic friend? To practice talking to yourself kindly? How about confronting your old, stale patterns and habits or creating a morning routine?

378

~~~

WOMAN TO WOMAN: DAILY MOTIVATIONAL QUOTES

December 6th

~~~

Once you start seeing people's hearts and spirits, instead of their appearance, you will find that they look totally different.

379

~~~

December 7th

~~

You really start to glow when you're happy mentally, physically, spiritually, and emotionally. So, go get yourself together and be happy.

380

~~

December 8th

~~~

Detox your timeline, your page, your home, your refrigerator, under your counters, your closet, your car, your phone, your life, and your mind. Start now.

381

~~~

December 9th

~~~

A person with no moral compass is a danger to anyone in his or her sphere. This person will intentionally work behind the scenes to destroy you and everything you've built to be happy. Don't let everyone in your space.

382

~~~

December 10th

~~~

May anyone in your life who
secretly gossips about you, puts
you down, or doesn't want
to see you win be replaced by
people who genuinely
support you and want
to see you happy.

383

~~~

December 11th

~

During transformation, you might feel like everything is falling apart. However, in reality, everything is coming together for your highest good. You're being pushed to evolve and to get out of your comfort zone so that you can live and experience your true greatness.

384

~

December 12th

~~~

Dear girl who sees her friends getting engaged, pregnant, married, moving into their first homes, posting pictures with their men, etc. and who feels like she's doing something wrong: STOP! Her season isn't your season. Your time will come.

385

~~~

December 13th

~~~

Everyone won't like the happy you. Some people enjoy the bitter you, so be careful about whom you share your highs and lows with.

386

~~~

December 14th

~~~

One reason people resist change is that they focus on what they are giving up instead of what they have to gain.

387

~~~

December 15th

~~~

Don't let the internet rush you.
No rich parents. No assistance.
No handouts. No favors.
No excuses. Straight hunger.
Straight ambition.
Straight hustle.

388

~~~

December 16th

~~~

The more disciplined you become, the more you realize that the areas in which you lacked control weren't worth the consequences.

389

~~~

December 17th

~

The body can literally reject someone's energy. Your anxiety will start acting up anytime bad energy disturbs your spirit. Listen to your body.

390

~

December 18th

~~~

Everything you want is waiting for you on the other side of consistency.

391

~~~

December 19th

~~~

Don't use social media less. Instead, use it more intentionally. Follow people who inspire and motivate you. Engage with experts from whom you can learn. Create genuine and positive connections. Stop mindlessly scrolling, complaining, hating, and engaging in negativity and bitterness.

392

~~~

December 20th

~~~

Aspire to be the woman who
wakes up and loves what she
does for a living,
who is spiritually secure
and financially stable.

393

~~~

December 21st

~~~

Seeing unhealthy patterns in your family and deciding that those patterns end with you and will not be passed down to future generations is an extremely brave and powerful choice.

394

~~~

December 22nd

~~~

Manifest the love you want.
Manifest the career you want.
Manifest the happiness you want.

395

~~~

December 23rd

~

Coming to terms with your amazingness really sets the tone for everything else in your life.

396

~

December 24th

~~~

Everything starts with you.
Start feeling worthy, valuable, and
deserving. When you do, you'll
receive the best that life has to offer.
When you love yourself, you glow
from within. You will attract people
who love and respect you.

397

~~~

December 25th

~~~

Merry Christmas. As you get older, you realize that you just want to be surrounded by good people-people who are good for you, good to you, and good for your soul.

398

~~~

December 26th

~~~

Your worth is non-negotiable.
Please don't let anyone at war
with themselves disturb
your peace.

399
~~~

December 27th

~

Every choice you make will place you at a certain point in life. Every heartbreak, every tear, every prayer that you felt wasn't answered—they have all actively conspired to lead you to this point in your life.

400

~

December 28th

~~~

Sometimes life is so subtle that you barely notice yourself walking through doors you once prayed would open.

401

~~~

December 29th

~

Be proud of yourself for how you handled this year. I don't know about you but I fought so many silent battles. I had to humble myself, wipe my own tears, and pat myself on the back. I'm sure you did the same. Be proud of YOU.

402

~

December 30th

~~~

Oh, she will! You aren't reading this by accident. Everything that has happened recently had to happen for you to grow. You are being prepared for amazing experiences.

403

~~~

December 31st

~

Quotes don't work unless you do. Hopefully, this year taught you how to mend your own heart, how to cope without people you thought would be in your life forever. This year taught you that no one can love you more than you love yourself. If you want to be successful, you have to do the work. No one will put you back on your feet. It's up to you. Quotes don't work unless you do! Happy New Year!

404

~

My Thoughts

WOMAN TO WOMAN: DAILY MOTIVATIONAL QUOTES

My Thoughts

WOMAN TO WOMAN: DAILY MOTIVATIONAL QUOTES

My Thoughts

WOMAN TO WOMAN: DAILY MOTIVATIONAL QUOTES

My Thoughts

WOMAN TO WOMAN: DAILY MOTIVATIONAL QUOTES

CPSIA information can be obtained
at www.ICGtesting.com
Printed in the USA
LVHW041504051120
670844LV00001B/73